QUICKLY, OVER THE WALL

QUICKLY,
OVER
THE WALL

POEMS

and Paintings by

Arnold Palmer

WAKE-BROOK HOUSE

LIBRARY OF CONGRESS CATALOG CARD : 66-20606

Printed in the United States of America

Designed by Hélène Géauque

A Handmade Book

Wake-Brook House, Coral Gables, Florida

Five hundred copies of this First Edition were printed.

This is copy number

Acknowledgments are extended to the following publications: THE BELOIT POETRY JOURNAL, THE BRIDGE, THE CARMEL PINE CONE-CYMBAL, CONTACT, THE CREATIVE REVIEW, CURLED WIRE CHRONICLE, THE DALHOUSIE REVIEW, FLAME, HILLTOPPER, KAYAK, MAINSTREAM, THE MISCELLANEOUS MAN, NEW VERSE, OLIVANT, POET AND CRITIC, FIFTH ANNUAL RELIGIOUS ARTS FESTIVAL, and the SAN FRANCISCO REVIEW.

Acknowledgment is also extended to Radio Station KPFA, over which many of these poems were read.

FOR CHARLENE

CONTENTS

Speech Without Words   13
Letter East   14
Boy on the Sand   15
Comment   18
Winter, Pacific Northwest, 1961   19
San Francisco: Morning of the Trial   20
        of a Conscientious Objector
1939   22
Too Actual Ever to Be a Symbol of   23
        Anything Other than What It Is
        the Sea Can Be Described Only
        in Its Own Terms
3 A.M.   25
Streaks of Dust   26
A Parting   31
Elegy   35
Expectations   36
Winter Sunset, Midwest   37
The Other Room   38
Yea, Though I Walk   40
Spring   41
Note from Arcata   42
Saturday Night   43
L'Art pour L'Art   44
When Spring Comes It Always   45
With My Son Stephen, at 4 A.M.   46
Morning   47
Of a Time   48
On the Side of the Trinity Alps   49
Bouquet   50

A Meeting   51
Afternoon   55
After the Rain   56
Not Even a General   57
Barracks #902   58
Something Like a Memory   60
Letter to a Soldier from His Wife   61
Stars Are a Symbol   62
The Last Prophet   64
Poem About Autumn   65

It's a long way to somewhere else.

THEODORE ROETHKE

SPEECH WITHOUT WORDS

They said the mad feel nothing.
They said I see nothing, am a piece
of wax, a pliable statue. They said
I do not recognize you
because I can not move
or say your name.
I will not tell them I looked
into a house where you are
placing red and yellow flowers
in your hair
where you whistle Mozart
teaching music to the air.
When they are washing me
they say I do not understand
do not know pain or any other thing.
I will not tell them I looked out once
from this sealed box
and saw a sky full of red and yellow suns
that spelled your name.
I will tell them nothing.

LETTER EAST

A chain saw cuts through autumn.
Behind me a dog howls at clouds
thickening in the woods. Leaves fall
their separate ways onto the dark grass.
I think of the sound sawdust makes
piling up on the red ground,
the earth silent forever.
I think of you in your neat winter house
as on another continent.
When you said I am not strong enough
and walked away
the air was full of leaves.
It is starting to rain.
The saw cuts the sun grain by red grain.
Soon it will snow in the mountains.

BOY ON THE SAND

A single amber streak plucks at the water
across the lake then another and another
in a moment a circus of yellow and black
and moonlight
swelling enormous this flooded space.
A green leaf floats into the night.

Alone on the warm sand, watching the city
across the lake startle to its other
its glittering shape, he thinks of naked girls
and jazz bands and Socrates' honest friends
picks a flat rock skipping it
far out toward the farthest light to see
the curling moon drip in its splashing path
like circus wheels
thinks of this morning along the graveyard wall
where, shrill as a parable, the wind whistled
at each slit and knothole
while he balanced himself with his hands flung out
and lept to the ground of tombstones propped
in the noiseless noiseless blue day sun.
Up and down, in and out of the long rows
he ran like a madman or the unstopped
feelings of the self damned
and running, felt a change
from the sullen grass
rise into his veins.

Quickly, over the wall to the black tar road
weaving breathless in the morning heat
he turned and whistled gently back
                              Goodbye, Goodbye
to that private world.

Forget the flow
Of wind and wall
Mounds of earth
A dusty curse
Upon your brain
Remember summer
Remember rain
Forget that houses
Are filled with pain
And will not change
Will never change
Remember spring rain.

Free as a falling leaf
he turns down the beach
seeing still the city on the lake
sparkle like history's heart beat
presses hard in his fingers
grains of sand that were rocks once
and shimmer now on the shadowless beach
and on his hand and up the empty hills
behind. Except for slow waves
there is no sound.
He slips out in his narrow wood boat
into a ring of tangled reeds alive

that scratch the sides lean over
and snap on his face, sharp
at the end of a season
but the smell is green and lingers.

Do not think of the hours
And years that will come
When love is undone
When you are undone
Push through the reeds
That flick your face
Remember this night
Remember this place
Slender reeds
Can make a trap
Will not suffice
To bring you back
Remember this night.

Far out on the water calm as stone
he coasts with the oars held up
drops of lake full of the moon
drip one by one from the silver oars
like the point of a star
or a falling moonlit autumn leaf.
A star rips loose red across the sky.
Beyond the first jutting pier
he hears a shriek of laughter
like a whisper in the nerve
jump at clicking neon buildings
tear and scatter the turning midnight.

COMMENT

Slowly turning to stone
I holler out
at the other statues
who look as if they are
going to smile.

Not wanting to offend
anyone
or, rather, myself
I turn the other way
where there are simple
hooks and hammers
wood boxes
          but this
(you will understand)
exists only
in my imagination.

WINTER, PACIFIC NORTHWEST, 1961

The clouds are stacked on the house
the moon is on top of the tree
wind blows wet silver through twigs
spun like spider webs
the radio delivers its message to the people
I wait for the dark hours to come.

SAN FRANCISCO : MORNING OF THE TRIAL
OF A CONSCIENTIOUS OBJECTOR

the infinitude of the private man

EMERSON

I

Gray discriminates for some
between the nightstick and the mallet.
Fog wet streets intersect and climb
bending through city lights
burning dim circles into the night.
Leaves drip on the cold sidewalk
of the Civic Square. A man hurries
down slow wind and fog horns.
In the courthouse alley a giant shadow
sits waiting like a wolf on a broken wall.

II

The air drifts quiet from the buildings
and statues and the Hall of Justice
where Rouault's Three Judges sit waiting.
The prisoner rolls his tongue in his dry mouth
pulls at his collar thinking
of the sharp edge of history where rulers
of men rattle like jingling silver, dancing coins
he remembers well enough
empty bells and ringing brass bands.

III

The black square he stands in
is infinite and not to be compared
with shadows . . .
His fingers learn grooves in the tile
brick wall connecting endless
as logic or law or San Francisco streets.
Through steel bars, far below, he sees
the bums on the corner
their orange crate fire shoots a shock of roses
at the gray morning air.

1939

The green sun
saturated wave
rises gracefully
out of
itself
like a civilization
towers superbly
for a moment
and is flattened
into the
green mass.

TOO ACTUAL EVER TO BE A SYMBOL OF ANYTHING OTHER THAN WHAT IT IS THE SEA CAN BE DESCRIBED ONLY IN ITS OWN TERMS

Inside the fine lit lounge the officers
are playing cards, drinking bourbon, talking.
Round white lights pour out of their portholes
and from their cabins.
Lights too burn in the open hatch
of the hold where the stacked soldiers
are asleep breathing in the smell
of each other's bodies, the nausea,
the dry factory heat of oil pumping machines.

An unused searchlight leans out
over the deck like a head.
It jerks sharply staring
into the North Atlantic wind slamming
against it and against everything
out on deck tonight.
Snouts of gun muzzles
stick out over the side
straight and undeniable as the black bar
of horizon against a gray dawn at sea
cold rigid steel
inflexible in its triumph.

Down down the sea

gigantic blocks of black waves
hurl themselves upward
crack against the prow
are sliced in two pushed under
are flipped over backward
out of context out of control
shoot out from the ship
sliding over and over itself
phosphorescent green white beautiful.
Underneath is darkness.

Six muted bells sound
all lights go out
a flash of water a block of steel.
There is no love out there.
There is no love here.
Cold steel cold sea
darkness.
It is night it is black
there are no lights anywhere.

3 A.M.

The rain has polished the night
into a black and white precision
while down on the unpeopled beach
the waves of the sea are breaking
against it.

STREAKS OF DUST

A biography of Mr. Stephen Miller, former Historian

Remaining pure in an impure world
is an exceedingly difficult task
and her white skin melted in the moonlight.

Possibly it was nothing
(you will regard it as such)
still, one wonders, somehow . . .

                        mixing
slipping one onto the other, piling
slabs of people and parties
and baseball lots, folding the
spring greens wet with poetry and awkward girls
with shining teeth and wondering eyes
compressing quietly into the snow white ice
filled valleys the toboggan sleds
and hockey games and grease loaded years
at the factory curving far into
the orange red gray green of autumn with
a wind of burnt leaves and the dying
immersed in yellow dust and little boy's dreams
of watered grapes in the icebox and sliced
oranges and ripe tomatoes bulging
and always the hollow sweating faces
of summer cities and the nightmares.

Her bronzed naked body clung
to his memory and he liked it
walking down the one street of this
gray Mexican town he knew she would be
waiting in her faded red dress, the sun burning
into her body and the cool smile
she would give him.

Crouching on the wet steel,
the lieutenant screaming words
I saw a solid chunk of white ocean stretch
up over the boat
You son bitch the foreign boy shrieked
and pushed the red brick high
through the numb winter air
and took his revenge on the laughter

lying in the blood
of his broken mouth and splintered nose

lying sprawled on the jagged crust
melted about his face
with warm blood

feeling the thick darkness pushing
into his face, twist it, drive
the long steel needles into it

only the needles keeping him alive
keeping the indifferent cells
from ice.

Driving down the long tar black road
beside his bride, Stephen thought
he'd have to stop being so selfish
What're you thinking, she said,
About your bright black hair, he lied
like he always did to her

Having seen them float onto
the delicate pools
of Detachment

having watched them drift
onto the tranquil waters of
Acceptance

he knew the meaning of fear
and kicked at one of the dull mounds of dust
at the side of the sun torn road

To write a history of the Mexican people
to write a history of people
this has never been done
                              must be done
the rest are charming lies

Her red dress was sucked in the hollow
of her thighs he wanted their warmth needed it
What's the matter, she said,
Me, he said,

and looked up at the million chips of clouds melting

in the rich night over Mt. Colima

The Great Historian must drink the blood of Caesar
with enthusiasm
                his mind a blade
of ice slicing the fat centuries
with the correct indifference
of a butcher knife
                incidents

What of the Generals the Heroes
standing defiant
their backs arched and proud
their swords stained with the blood
of their people
                what of Cortez
covered with gore and blessed
by the cross
                (O where was the bléssed man ripped from it?)

Come by me tonight

Would you come by me tonight

Looking into the past, he said,
is trying to see through stained glass
and opened his office window
and looked out into the dusk
watching the white lights begin
to appear like grains of salt
sprinkled on black cloth

The smell of poverty and polished ladies
the breathing of seven million
people mixed with the muffled and far
away auto horns and street cars
spread through the evening air sticking
to the sides of buildings, groping
at the windows and reminded Mr. Miller
it was time to go home.

A PARTING

Here the crawling vines scratch the antique day
as if we were ants buried in a jungle of grass
outside your well defined house
although no poem or image will ever dissect
Reason as I now would.

You walk through it for the first time
in your life with a look of certain confidence
not thinking anymore of a chipped Greek column
or an olive tree shedding butterflies
or these spiked unnumbered vines.

Strange I think but not for you now
seeing a bright legend where I see none
finding in an archaic language
a new and facile tongue.

ELEGY

Loaded with pity and afraid like the rest
he wondered once before it
blotted out the laughter
squashed the last flickering
of revolt like a tank crams
a human enemy into the hard coffin
of his own bones
                    insatiable
hammered precision into the nerves
like an adding machine wringing routine
into the once nimble fingers
and pronounced him acceptable.

Now, when sweat pries loose from
a nightmare and loneliness eats at his stomach
like a tapeworm
he remembers with the passionate
indifference of the man on the street
that there will be no monuments.

EXPECTATIONS

Primed on benzedrine
guarding the green lawn

the caged day
scrapes in at the dawn
and blinds the night
with light with light

and will find him there
before very long.

WINTER SUNSET, MIDWEST

Watching the red come through empty branches
I think of stairs that lead nowhere
dying elm trees hypocrite speeches.
These dead branches are rusty spikes
stuck into the heart of this town
of bad will and big bank rolls.
I go up the stairs to my house and find
it is the wrong house at the wrong time of day.
I ask a passing man with a white silk scarf
over his face if by chance he has any news.
He corrects his hat adjusts his watch
which has stopped and hurries on.
The sun sinks under my feet.
I can not find a face without clocks
dead trees without echo stairs that end
or your steady breathing next to my ear.

THE OTHER ROOM

He goes in the other room sits in the armchair
and looks out of the window
a brown knit scarf about his neck.
Outside the wind is blowing the last skeleton leaves
down the autumn street into gutters
lawns doorways.
A car passes.
Gusts of sand lift off the vacant lot
across the street where they've begun
another building.
The sand lifts twisted
in the shifting air is laid down
is picked up again
a world in pantomime.
This is the last time I'll see that.
This is how it is.
Somewhere from the back of the house comes
a muffled ticking like a distant drum tap.
The wind pulls at the loose shingles they rattle
against each other knock on the roof
the door shakes.

He sits in the armchair his thin fingers tracing flower
patterns erased to a dull crust.
Late yellow sun drifts in through the window
marking shafts of afternoon
cut by the cross of window bars
on the rug the floor an old book case.
He sits in the chair
an old man.
It's been a long day.

YEA, THOUGH I WALK

"'Yea, though I walk
through the valley
of the shadow . . .
I will fear no evil;
for Thou art with me.'"

"But when one of us is dead,
I will be alone," she said.

"It is God who will be with you, not I."

"Then I will be alone," she said;
"not all the gods in the sky
or all the devils on earth
will comfort me without you."

"God is the Great Comforter,
you will not weep with loneliness.
He is Everywhere
and Always
and Everything.
No one is ever really dead."

"I will be alone," she said.

SPRING

*Remember man, from dust thou come
and to dust thou shalt return.*

Green wheat reels in yellow sun
watch cool gold pools and waterfalls
strike against the brittle rocks
fill the blue and crackling air
with stalks of form line and leaves
smell the green wet fist of spring
punch down the dead compel the dove
bend back the olive branch
       Remember
love from dust thou art lovely
as wind in a poplar tree
a shouting bush a lilac
then touch these yellow shafts
melting shadows black as coal
dead as ice twisting shape of moving
years rotting apples smashed to earth
then feel beneath us biting roots
clutch like touching hands
the soft and timeless dark
then look the tangled
blue slate grass whirls
everywhere and colors leap
within your eyes
     O love
the day lies deep upon the land
the dust of summer stirs.

NOTE FROM ARCATA

Wearing his wound like a carnation
in his lapel
and fingering his famous pipe
the Professional was shocked
to see street lights dance
down the wet pavement of this
smallest town on earth
and was last seen
hastily hopping the one train
out.

SATURDAY NIGHT

Euclid alone has looked on Beauty bare.
EDNA ST. VINCENT MILLAY

She rolls down her stockings carefully
to avoid any runs.
I stand in the corner, watching.
She starts in on the zipper.
Having decided to play it casual
I lean over the dresser.
"Need any help?" I magnanimously ask.
She smiles in a certain
non-Euclidian way.
"Thanks a lot," she says.
"I always did like a gentleman."

L'ART POUR L'ART

The vanilla ice cream white
as a winter window pane
can't help being beautiful (even
with the fat lady shoveling it in
to her ever expectant mouth.

WHEN SPRING COMES IT'S ALWAYS

When spring comes it's always now.
The ponds and puddles
of brown rain water ripple in the green wind
drifting through spring green
and little boys march through
every small lake they can find —
and all for the first time
it's always the first time in spring
it's always now.

WITH MY SON, STEPHEN, AT 4 A.M.

I sit in the quiet.
It is morning.
I am reading an anthology.
My family and friends
are long asleep.
If I listen carefully
I can imagine
their regular breathing.
Suddenly Stephen
hollers out
DON'T
NO
DON'T DO IT
NO DON'T
I talk to him
rub his head
bring him water
put the covers
back in place.
Futile empty
awkward gestures
to keep me
from wondering
what it is
I have done.

MORNING

The cream clouds
Burst
    in my
    coffee cup
Drowning
    the black
    with a
    beige
Conquest

OF A TIME

Under the table
under that mountain
the band is playing
a Viennese waltz
while you amuse yourself
and he
(the waiter, the man in the rain)
makes a decision
I pour
pausing to contemplate
the Universe
and wonder whatever became
of the good old days.

ON THE SIDE OF THE TRINITY ALPS

The house is bending under the rain.
I stare out the window at the lightning
and feel the house shake
with every crack of thunder.
My daughter, Charna, asks me to turn it off.
I understand it's a long way down.

BOUQUET

Every time I try to sleep
the roses insist
on coming in
through the window
whereupon they make such a ruckus
in our always cluttered house
I can't close my eyes
until I gather them up one by one
and give them to my wife
who says Yes Yes thank you very much.

A MEETING

(for Charlene)

Because you are not loud like a dying city
but quiet as the summer trees showered
with moonlight in the still
hours before dawn

Because you are new like peeled oranges
and real as the green leaves on a strawberry bush
I came to your warmth
                    ominous and fearful
as a cold winter morning with the sun glistening

There was no breath in the air
and only silence

with a gradual shift of the earth.

David Palmer
1/25/53

AFTERNOON

Two small girls about seven years old
rollerskate under the window of our second story
apartment. Their wheels click on the cracks
at regular intervals and grind over holes
and pebbles on the sidewalk. Looking down
I see thin legs shoot out from
outgrown skirts, bare arms grab
at the air to give balance or speed
voices jumble into each other, oblivious
screaming accomplishment, scorn or approval
as they skate past me into the wholly beautiful
sun filled and otherwise quiet day.

Realizing I should be doing something else
I turn back into our room
and see on the couch a newspaper headline
of the approaching war.

AFTER THE RAIN

It was a funny thing watching the old
man across the street he must have been
over eighty standing in front of a
Rexall Drug Store on the curb next to
the gutter we stood across the street
kitty corner from him watching for some
reason he was just standing there on his
right leg you could see the left leg was
artificial the way he had it
pushed out away from him contemptuous
the top of it bulging against his pants
he was looking over at us but blank
like he was looking at nothing at all
the way his hock shop suit fell over
his bent spine like a cloak showed he had
it a long time he stood there looking
then crumbled all of a sudden his face
splashing hard on the shallow water in
the gutter we ran across the street to
him people started sticking together
right away we rolled him over so he
wouldn't drown his faded blue white eyes
stared up and hit you right in the face if
you looked at him the crowd fell back a little
I reached down to close his eyes with my fingers
but I didn't.

NOT EVEN A GENERAL

You can't puncture the blue
out of the sky (not even
with a cannon
on a Sunday) but they're
still trying

BARRACKS #902

Everything is quiet except the deep heavy breathing
of exhausted men asleep.
A light from somewhere outside cuts into the black
with ironic calm moving changing shapes.
Two steel rows of fifty double cots mark uniform
shadows on the mop soaked floor, the worn boots
and shoes laced tight, shined uniform for instant
inspection.
Shadows of blue metal rifles lined ordered in the
quiet
rifle rack slant against the cracked wood wall
where twin measured columns of domed helmets
and rigid stuffed field packs lay
bayonets turned upward glinting bright and silent
in silent moonlight. This room is an abstract
painting
in black and white and these men are inside it.
Beside each steel cot belts, neckties, pressed and
buttoned
uniforms hang over gray faces almost the same
too tired now for anger or questions.
The man in the last lower cot is propped up
against a steel bar to keep from coughing.
In three or four days he will be dead.
Somebody stirs upstairs, fumbles with his boots
clomps across the rutted wood floor and down
the long steps, his boot laces clicking behind.

Half asleep he moves to the water fountain
gulps to drink and coughs over and over again.
Slower, more deliberate, louder,
he goes upstairs to his cot.
Nobody stirs now nobody moves
they will come soon enough. Timeless
tomorrow it will begin again.

SOMETHING LIKE A MEMORY

The scarred mountains carve the sky into grotesque
beauty reminding us of our heritage. Out here
where the air is caught between two cliffs
and a lone jay bird seems suspended we remember
quietly the tempo of another time . . .

Tomorrow we will again go about our business
and the moment of defiance conjectured
something like a memory
while the sun pushes down through our hidden
paradise twisting the few scattered leaves
like claws into dust.

LETTER TO A SOLDIER FROM HIS WIFE

Moonlight falls through the window of our room
covering the floor and the bed like a bandage
shaping the chain and light bulb that hangs there
the chair and shoes and empty table.
The pictures you hung on the wall are scattered
the same as if nothing had happened.
I have been too long in our lone bed
to reach out and think to find you
still, at night, I sometimes deceive myself.
There is a crack in the window where the light
glitters, vibrating like a sharp diamond.
Outside, the tree you listened for is blowing leaves
over the yard hitting the shingles of the roof
bending far enough to break in the storms
tearing the rocks off the coast these months.
The strong wood fence you built is beginning
to split and flap in the wind.
Frozen Europe holds you folded in an ice ditch.
Listening to snows from the north
what can you dream of me, of leaves
on the face of the year?
It is five o'clock in the long silence
I wait for the low morning fog.

STARS ARE A SYMBOL

We are not so far as to recognize
a single consequence of a starlit
place where nevertheless occasional lights
break the night into a conglomerate
of whatever it is we are to believe in.

The black walled concrete side streets at four
o'clock in the morning of this twentieth century
city are everywhere a foreshadow, a vatic silence
which does not remember your name, or know your image.

We are not so far as to recognize
whatever it is we are.

Walking down it, a caricature of a circus clown
torn with grief but like Caesar, knowing
the ancient thrill of vengeance
and thus the history
of a dead species.

                        We are not so far as to
recognize
yet the pictures your brain flashes on the screen
smelling the garbage blossoming out of a billion
ash cans alleys smokestacks factories garages gutters
houses doorways makes you wonder why you can not
reach up and pull airproof noiseproof tight the window
of Plato's cave.

Whatever it was we were supposed to remember
when the time came
                    (the splintered flash-back
of somebody's life, the long winter hikes through
a solid white universe, the violent splash of blue
red autumn and the deep wet earth smell of spring rain
the almost white dust settling on a gray moon
filled road just after dusk, the sun blowing gold off
a million leaves and rocks on that mountain
you were always going to come back to)
whatever it was we were supposed to remember
when the time came
somehow none of it spreads through your brain
numbing the hour somehow it doesn't work.
The one alternative to illusion you can see
on this your hometown your own street between
the inarticulate shadows of factory buildings rotting
fences squashed tin cans broken windows parked cars
underneath the streamlined skyscraping steel you can see
the one alternative to illusion the price of power
you can see the one alternative here.

We are not so far as to recognize whatever it is
yet the blue white points piercing the night
give cause to wonder that between us
there is O a possibility
of something other than a steel bayonet pressing
against our windpipe the sound of a triumphant maniac
scratching our tomorrow's final illegible history.

THE LAST PROPHET

I have hurled my words at the towns and the faces but they move only as they have always moved and do not hear me. I have called to my brothers on the road gang and I have called to my sisters at the dances but the picks will not cease spatting the rocks into rubble, nor the juke-box stop whirling for an instant. There is only the noise and the wind burning out faces and towns into dust and no one will hear me.

I have called out in a clear voice across the empty valleys and lone roads leading into the orange sunset. I have stood at the top of the mountains and shouted out through the clean silent air where the sky is, but there is only the wind, burning

POEM ABOUT AUTUMN

While you are warm with sleep
breathing softly in the cool blue air
of this flamboyant dawn
I sit on this side of the bed watching
you almost smile in some dream perhaps
and I wonder if you remember that last
autumn day, the prow of our boat slicing
the green layers open crushing the yellow
streaks of sun with its wooden weight
the sails stretching white into the roaring
sky, the wind wild and heavy as an iron wall
your face wet with the cold spray
red lips stung brilliant
                        O your hair light
as laughter
                 we watched the trail of flattened
waves widen out behind while far off
miniature towns fell unreal into the
lead horizon
             and slowly
with the quiet authority of something
not quite inevitable the solid block
of day chipped piece by piece
and crumbled at last into the billion
multicolored grains of late autumn dusk

The hour to return or be lost

We brought our boat in between the rocks
to safe harbor and the night heavy
with moisture thick with the smell
of the lake and seaweed alone we walked
through moonlight down the white beach
listening to waves spill on the sand
the evening air move beautiful against
dying leaves on the shore their twisting
shadows hitting down on our path with the weight
of raindrops
                    we, then, trying
to hold the sharp liquid moonlight motionless
on the water, trying to bend time to us —
time straight as a steel cliff and jagged —
thinking that final autumn the birth
of the first spring and immortal as morning

Here, now in this room, watching your white
flesh soften with sleep as this strange
concrete day pushes in through our window
I hear the soldiers marching in the streets
I feel the restless cracking of the stones.